Let Freedom Ring

Dolley Madison

First Lady

by Barbara Witteman

Consultants:
Kristin Celello, Associate Editor
Amy Minton, Associate Editor
The Dolley Madison Project, University of Virginia

Bridgestone Books
an imprint of Capstone Press
Mankato, Minnesota

Bridgestone Books are published by Capstone Press
151 Good Counsel Drive, PO Box 669, Mankato, Minnesota 56002
http://www.capstone-press.com

Library of Congress Cataloging-in-Publication Data
Witteman, Barbara.
   Dolley Madison: First Lady/by Barbara Witteman.
   p. cm.—(Let freedom ring)
   Summary: A biography of Dolley Madison, wife of the fourth president of the United States, from her Quaker childhood to her roles as a hostess for Thomas Jefferson, First Lady, and heroine in the War of 1812.
   Includes bibliographical references and index.
   ISBN 0-7368-1551-1 (hardcover)
   1. Madison, Dolley, 1768–1849—Juvenile literature. 2. Presidents' spouses—United States—Biography—Juvenile literature. [1. Madison, Dolley, 1768-1849. 2. First ladies. 3. Women—Biography.] I. Title. II. Series.
E342.1 .W58 2003
973.5'1'092—dc21   2002012065

Editorial Credits
Rebecca Glaser, editor; Kia Adams, series designer; Juliette Peters, book designer;
   Kelly Garvin, photo researcher; Karen Risch, product planning editor

Photo Credits
Courtesy of Montpelier Museum/Philip Beaurline, 42
Courtesy of Woodmere China/photo taken by Capstone Press/Gary Sundermeyer,
   cover (inset), 43
Greensboro Historical Museum, Greensboro, N.C., 25, 36
Hulton Archive by Getty Images, cover (main photo), 5, 13, 15, 19, 35
Interstate Brands West Corporation/photo taken by Capstone Press/Gary Sundermeyer, 41
Library of Congress, 31
Louise and Alan Sellars Collection of Art by American Women, 21
The Library of Virginia, 9
North Wind Picture Archives, 10, 27, 28, 38
Stock Montage, Inc., 7, 16, 22

The author dedicates this book to her daughter, Anne.

1   2   3   4   5   6   08   07   06   05   04   03

Table of Contents

Chapter One

Dolley Madison

In 1812, the United States declared war on Great Britain. The United States had won independence from Great Britain after the Revolutionary War (1775–1783). But relations between Great Britain and the new nation were not good. Americans were upset about Great Britain's practice of taking American sailors and forcing them to serve on British ships. Great Britain blocked United States trade so Americans could not sell their goods in Europe.

After two years of war, the British were threatening to attack the new nation's capital, Washington, D.C. In August 1814, President James Madison was away from Washington, D.C., encouraging the U.S. Army troops. The first lady, Dolley Madison, was at home in the President's

Dolley Madison was first lady during the War of 1812.

House, later called the White House. Dolley anxiously waited for news from her husband. She received a note from him telling her to pack everything she could and to save government papers.

Dolley prepared to leave. She had several trunks packed with James' papers. When she saw the portrait of George Washington on the wall, she decided to save it. Dolley told servants to break the frame and roll up the canvas. She gave the portrait to two passing men, Robert DePeyster and Jacob Barker, who carried it to safety. Dolley then escaped to a friend's house outside the city.

Not only was Dolley Madison a brave woman, but she was also a charming and graceful first lady. People looked to Dolley for fashion trends and social customs. During the early 1800s, she was one of the most popular people in Washington, D.C.

Dolley's parents would never have guessed that she would become so popular. As a young girl, Dolley had worn plain gray dresses like other people of the Quaker faith.

Dolley saved important government papers just before an attack
on the President's House in 1814.

Chapter Two

Early Life

Dolley Payne was born on May 20, 1768, in what is today Guilford County, North Carolina. Dolley's parents, John and Mary Coles Payne, lived in the state for a short time. Dolley was their oldest daughter and one of nine children. The family moved to Virginia when Dolley was young. The family belonged to the Society of Friends, whose members also are known as Quakers.

Dolley's father owned a Virginia plantation. He also owned slaves. He eventually freed his slaves because Quakers believed owning slaves was wrong. They believed that all people were equal. The family moved to Philadelphia, Pennsylvania, in July 1783, after John quit farming.

Legend has it that Dolley's family lived for a while at Scotchtown, a plantation in Virginia.

Quakers

Members of the Society of Friends are commonly known as Quakers. In 1650, George Fox founded the society in England. In colonial America, many Quakers settled in Pennsylvania. They were opposed to war. They sent both boys and girls to school at a time when few girls were educated. Quaker clothing was plain. Quakers were opposed to slavery. They helped many slaves escape in the nineteenth century.

Today, Quakers have many of the same beliefs they had in the past. They are a peaceful people who do not support war. They also believe that God lives in people's hearts. Quakers today continue to dress simply and remain humble.

Life in Philadelphia

John bought a starch-making business in Philadelphia. People put starch on their clothes to make them stiffer and to remove wrinkles. John did not know how to run a business, and he lost all of his money. His failure depressed him, and his health began to decline.

A lawyer named John Todd asked Dolley to marry him. She first said no, but later changed her mind. They married in a Quaker meetinghouse on January 7, 1790.

Dolley and her husband enjoyed their life in Philadelphia and began to raise a family. Their first child, John Payne Todd, was born on February 29, 1792. They called him Payne. Their second child, William Temple Todd, was born on July 4, 1793.

After Dolley's father died, her mother turned the Payne home into a boardinghouse so she could support her family. Philadelphia was the capital of the United States, and government men needed places to stay and eat meals. Famous people such as Aaron Burr, who later became vice president, and Thomas Jefferson, third U.S. president, stayed at the Payne boardinghouse.

Yellow Fever

During the hot and humid summer of 1793, an outbreak of yellow fever spread across Philadelphia. This disease brought sudden fever, headaches, and bleeding. It sometimes turned people's skin yellow. Doctors did not know how to treat the disease, and more than 4,000 people in the Philadelphia area died that summer.

At the time, people thought the disease was contagious. They quit talking to each other and would not shake hands. They did not know that virus-carrying mosquitoes spread the disease. People left Philadelphia to live in the country. They mistakenly thought they would be safe there.

Dolley's husband, John, took his family to the country and then returned to the city. He took care of his sick parents, who had yellow fever. He wrote wills for people who were dying from the fever. When John himself became sick, he went to see Dolley in the country. He died in October 1793. Baby William had been sick and died the same month. Dolley returned with 2-year-old Payne to Philadelphia.

One year after her son William's death, Dolley had this miniature of herself painted.

Chapter Three

A New Husband

In May 1794, Aaron Burr told Dolley that James Madison wanted to meet her. Dolley was surprised that a famous man like James wanted to meet her. James had written much of the U.S. Constitution. James was 17 years older than Dolley. Following their first meeting, he often came to see her. Later that year, he asked Dolley to marry him.

Dolley took a long time to think about marrying James. Friends and relatives talked about the couple. They encouraged Dolley to marry James. According to one story, Martha Washington talked to Dolley about James. Martha told Dolley that she and President Washington thought James was a good man. After much thought, Dolley agreed to marry James.

James Madison married Dolley Todd. He later became the fourth president of the United States.

The Madisons' Wedding

Dolley and James married on September 15, 1794. They traveled to several places on their month-long honeymoon. Dolley's son Payne went with them. At that time, it was common for people to travel with the bridal couple. The bridal couple often visited friends and family on their honeymoons.

After their honeymoon, the Madisons stayed for a short time at James' Virginia plantation, called

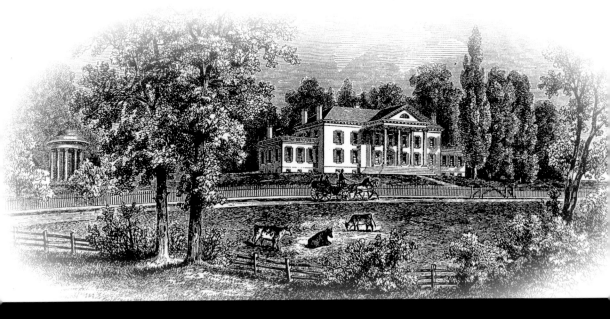

Montpelier, a plantation in Virginia, was the Madisons' home.

Montpelier. Because James was a congressman, they soon moved to Philadelphia, where Congress met.

Philadelphia and Montpelier

As the capital of the United States, Philadelphia was a social center for the new country. Wealthy people hosted formal dances and dinners in their homes.

Dolley enjoyed life in Philadelphia. She had a group of female friends. She also went to parties with James. Dolley was outgoing and James was quiet, but they got along well.

In 1797, James' term in Congress was over. The Madisons moved back to Montpelier. James grew tobacco and clover on his plantation. Dolley oversaw household production, including sewing clothes and growing vegetables to eat. Slaves on the plantation helped with both the farming and household duties.

The Madisons Move to Washington, D.C.

In 1790, the U.S. Congress decided to make a permanent capital. Congress had previously met both in New York and Philadelphia. President George Washington chose a site on the Potomac River between Virginia and Maryland. A commission planned the new capital and named it Washington after the first president. In 1800, Washington, D.C., became the permanent capital of the United States.

Thomas Jefferson won the presidential election of 1800. Jefferson was the Madisons' good friend and neighbor in Virginia. Jefferson asked James to be his secretary of state. James agreed. He became a member of the president's cabinet and worked with the president on foreign policy.

Housing was hard to find in Washington. The Madisons lived with Jefferson for about a month in the President's House while they looked for a house. Some people accused Jefferson of taking in boarders.

Early Washington was not a pleasant place. Houses were built among swamps, fields, and trees. The President's House was not finished. Jefferson brought his own furniture.

Hostess Dolley

Jefferson's wife had died before he became president. His two daughters lived in Virginia with their own families. Jefferson needed a hostess to help him plan dinners and parties. He asked Dolley if she would help, and she agreed.

Dolley was a perfect hostess. She was kind to everyone. Dolley spoke to every guest at parties. She made sure there was good food to eat. She arranged after-dinner entertainment.

Dolley also hosted dinners and parties at her and James' house. She even invited people who disagreed with her husband's political ideas. James explained his beliefs about government at these dinners.

Thomas Jefferson was the third president of the United States. Because Jefferson's wife had died, Dolley served as Jefferson's hostess.

Chapter Four

Living in the President's House

James ran for president in 1808 and won. On March 4, 1809, James took the oath of office. That evening, the Madisons went to a special dance held in their honor called the inaugural ball. This was the first inaugural ball held for a president. The Madisons moved into the President's House.

Dolley planned her and James' social lives and organized their dinners. She also tended to family matters. James said that Dolley was "the greatest blessing of my life."

Dolley's Fashions

People in America watched Dolley. They wanted to see what she wore. They talked about her hairstyles and jewelry. Dolley liked dresses that were cut low in the front with high waistlines and straight skirts.

A grand inaugural ball was held for James and Dolley Madison when James became president.

The President's House

The President's House, pictured below, was finished in 1800. John and Abigail Adams, the second president and his wife, were the first people to live there. The house had not been ready when George Washington was president. The house had to be rebuilt after the British burned it during the War of 1812. It then was called the Executive Mansion. Because the outside walls were painted white, people began to call it the White House. The name became official in 1902.

This fashion was called the Empire style. She wore hats called turbans that matched her dresses. Dolley dressed up for dinners, held at 4:00 in the afternoon.

Dolley did not always wear fancy clothes. During the day, she wore simple gray dresses. Large, white aprons covered her dresses. She also wore a kerchief around her neck.

Political Views

James belonged to the Democratic-Republican Party. The Democratic-Republicans opposed the Federalist Party, which wanted a strong federal government controlled by the upper class. The Democratic-Republicans wanted a limited national government, controlled by landholders, regardless of class. Dolley agreed with her husband on most political issues.

Entertaining in Washington

On Wednesday nights, Dolley organized receptions called "drawing rooms." No one needed an invitation. Dolley made all of her guests feel welcome. She always remembered everyone's names. Dolley often carried the book *Don Quixote* with her and talked about it to start conversation if people were too quiet. She also carried a box of snuff, or powdered tobacco. She offered snuff to her guests and occasionally took a pinch herself. James liked these informal parties because he could come and go as he pleased.

Dolley's dinners in the President's House were well known. They included good food, wines, cake, macaroons, fruit, nuts, and ice cream. She also served a warm dessert called Baked Alaska, made with ice cream and cake. Dolley sat at the head of the table and served food. Although a president normally sat at the head of the table, James sat at the side of the table. Dolley invited members of every political party to her dinners.

Decorating the President's House

The President's House did not have much furniture when Dolley and James moved there. Congress gave Dolley money to furnish the President's House.

Dolley worked with Benjamin Latrobe, an architect and decorator. He had designed the inside of the Capitol building. They bought chairs,

Dolley's Fashions

Many people in Washington, D.C., noticed Dolley's fashions. Margaret Bayard Smith was a close friend of Dolley Madison and was her first biographer. In a letter, she described the dress Dolley wore to James' inaugural ball in 1809.

"She looked like a queen. She had on a pale buff-colored velvet, made plain, with a very long train . . . [She also wore] a beautiful pearl necklace, earrings and bracelet. Her headdress was a turban of the same coloured velvet and white satin (from Paris) with two superb plumes, the bird of paradise feathers."

Two of Dolley's dresses, including the one shown at right, are displayed at the Greensboro Historical Museum in North Carolina.

candelabra, mirrors, china, and a small piano. Dolley picked out red velvet curtains and yellow satin curtains. She hung portraits of the first three U.S. presidents in her new home.

Chapter Five

The War of 1812

James' first term as president ended in 1812. He ran for reelection. DeWitt Clinton ran against him. James was reelected. Clinton said that he could have defeated James alone but not both James and Dolley. Dolley was the most popular person in Washington, D.C.

America Goes to War

In 1812, some people in the United States wanted war with Great Britain. Great Britain was not treating the United States fairly. British ships stopped American ships from trading. The Americans accused the British of taking American sailors and making them work on British ships. The British gave weapons to American Indians in the West so the Indians could fight the settlers.

America declared war on Great Britain on June 18, 1812. The British had a large army of well-trained men.

British ships blocked American ships from trading goods with other countries. This practice was one cause of the War of 1812.

The U.S. Army had only 7,000 poorly prepared men. Battles were fought on both water and land. The war went on for about two years. Dolley gave parties to celebrate American victories.

In August 1814, the British threatened to attack the capital. People thought the Americans would lose. James went to encourage the American soldiers. He told Dolley to stay at the President's House until his return.

The British burned the city of Washington, D.C., in August 1814.

On August 24, the British met the American forces at Bladensburg, Maryland. From there, James wrote a note to Dolley, telling her to be ready to leave on a minute's notice.

The Burning of Washington

In the President's House, Dolley could hear the cannons firing. The 100 men who were supposed to guard the house had disappeared. Dolley ordered a wagon brought to the house. The servants loaded up important papers, silver, a clock, and some curtains. A messenger arrived and told everyone to leave. They had to leave without eating dinner.

Dolley wanted to save the large picture of George Washington, but the frame was screwed into the wall. To save time, Dolley had servants break the frame and remove the painted canvas. She gave the rolled up portrait to two passing men. They took it to safety.

Dolley then fled the city with only her maid for company. She did not plan where to go. No record proves where she stayed, but she probably went to friends' houses in Virginia.

What She Was Thinking

Dolley wrote to one of her sisters as Washington was about to be attacked. "Will you believe it, my sister? We have had a battle . . . and here I am still, within sound of cannon! Mr. Madison comes not. May God protect us! . . . Our kind friend, Mr. Carroll, has come to hasten my departure, and is [very angry] with me, because I insist on waiting until the large picture of General Washington is secured, and it requires to be unscrewed from the wall. This process was found too tedious for these perilous moments; I have ordered the frame to be broken, and the canvas taken out. It is done!"

The British troops arrived that evening after Dolley left. They set fire to the Capitol. Flying sparks burned many of the area's homes. At the President's House, the British found the table set for dinner. They ate and then set fire to the house. The glare from the fires could be seen for 40 miles (64 kilometers).

The next day, a terrible storm hit the city. Wind blew off roofs, and rain fell in torrents. The storm put out the fires and kept the British from attacking the city again.

After the attack, James and Dolley returned to Washington, D.C. But only the outside walls of the President's House remained. A man named Mr. Tayloe let the Madisons live in his Octagon House.

The end of the war was near. Baltimore, Maryland, withstood a British attack. The British fleet surrendered to the U.S. Navy on Lake Champlain between Vermont and New York. The two sides signed a peace treaty at Ghent, in what is now Belgium,

Dolley and James Madison stayed at the oddly-shaped Octagon House for awhile after the President's House burned.

on December 24, 1814. But news of the treaty did not reach the southern states, and the last battle of the war was fought at New Orleans in early 1815. American forces won the battle.

Normal Life Returns to Washington, D.C.

Life returned to normal. Although the President's House was eventually rebuilt, it was not done in time for James and Dolley to live there again. Dolley entertained in the evenings.

According to some stories, Dolley fed her macaw, a type of parrot, by a window. Crowds gathered every day to watch this bird. The macaw repeated French phrases it had learned from the Madisons' French servant.

In October 1815, Dolley helped start a home for orphans. She was asked to be its "directoress." Dolley spent the winter helping to make clothes for the children. She also donated money and a cow.

James' term as president ended in March 1817 when James Monroe became the next president. Many farewell parties were held for Dolley and James over the next month. Dolley and James then moved to their home at Montpelier.

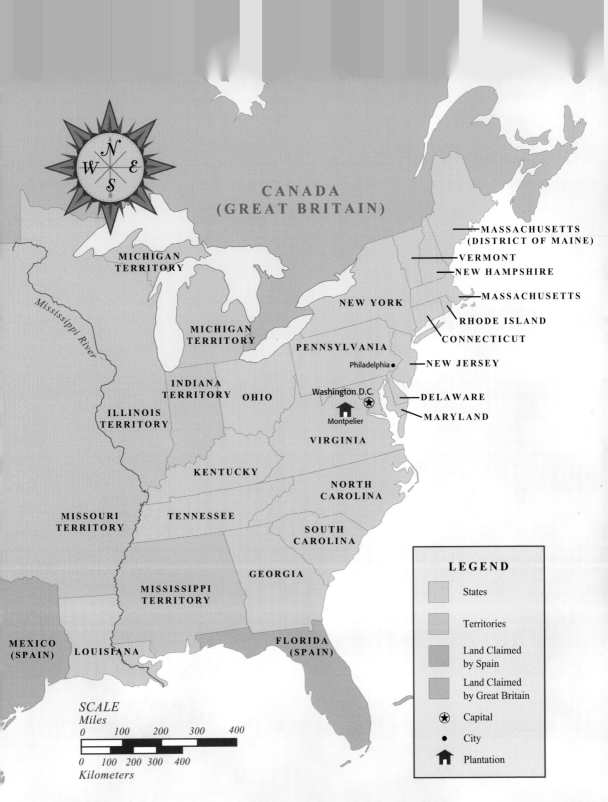

CANADA
(GREAT BRITAIN)

MASSACHUSETTS
(DISTRICT OF MAINE)

VERMONT

NEW HAMPSHIRE

MASSACHUSETTS

RHODE ISLAND

CONNECTICUT

NEW JERSEY

DELAWARE

MARYLAND

MICHIGAN
TERRITORY

MICHIGAN
TERRITORY

NEW YORK

PENNSYLVANIA

Philadelphia

Washington D.C.

Montpelier

INDIANA
TERRITORY

OHIO

ILLINOIS
TERRITORY

VIRGINIA

KENTUCKY

MISSOURI
TERRITORY

TENNESSEE

NORTH
CAROLINA

SOUTH
CAROLINA

GEORGIA

MISSISSIPPI
TERRITORY

MEXICO
(SPAIN)

LOUISIANA

FLORIDA
(SPAIN)

Mississippi River

LEGEND

States

Territories

Land Claimed
by Spain

Land Claimed
by Great Britain

Capital

City

Plantation

SCALE
Miles

0   100   200   300   400

0   100 200 300 400
Kilometers

Chapter Six

Later Years

Dolley and James returned home to Montpelier. They entertained many visitors there. James, then 66 years old, began farming again on the plantation.

Life at Montpelier

James and Dolley organized his political papers. James had notes of the Constitutional Convention, which had met in secret sessions. He wanted to sell them so Dolley would have money after he died. James also thought historians could use them.

Dolley took care of James when he was sick. He suffered often from rheumatism, a disease that causes the joints and muscles to become swollen and painful. When James got tired, Dolley would write for him.

Dolley's later years were spent at Montpelier and in Washington, D.C.

Dolley's son, Payne, added to his parents' worries about money. Now in his 20s, he spent most of his time gambling and drinking. When he could not pay for these activities, he borrowed money. James paid some of Payne's gambling and drinking debts, but Payne still went to debtor's prison twice. In early America, people with large debts were put in prison until they could pay their bills. James always helped Payne and paid his bills. Dolley did

Dolley's niece Anna (left) lived with Dolley after James died.

not know that James paid them. Payne never learned his lesson. He kept gambling and drinking.

James died on June 28, 1836. The Madisons had been married for 42 years. Dolley worked to get his papers published. In April 1837, Congress bought the first three volumes for $30,000.

Dolley Returns to Washington, D.C.

Dolley was lonely after James died. Her niece Anna Payne came to live with her. In 1837, about one year after James died, Dolley and Anna moved to Washington, D.C. The house where Dolley and Anna lived was on Lafayette Square, near the White House. Dolley enjoyed seeing her Washington friends again. She held receptions, and most of the people who visited the president also went across the street to see her.

Dolley left Payne in charge of Montpelier. But Payne did not take good care of the plantation. He did not know how to run a plantation. Dolley and Anna moved several times between Montpelier and Washington, D.C. But Dolley did not know how to run a plantation either. In August 1844, she sold Montpelier to pay bills.

Telegraph

Samuel Morse invented the telegraph. A line was built between Baltimore and Washington, D.C., in 1844. Dolley was in the Capitol when the first message arrived from a woman in Baltimore on May 24 that year. Morse asked Dolley to send the second message. She sent it to one of her cousins in Baltimore. It read, "Message from Mrs. Madison. She sends her love to Mrs. Wethered."

Money Problems

Dolley tried to get more of James' papers published. She contacted private publishers for two years. She then offered the papers to Congress. The lawmakers were busy because the United States was at war with Mexico. Finally, in 1847, Congress agreed to buy the rest of the papers to help Dolley. She received a total of $25,000. Most of the money was put in a trust. Only Dolley could spend the money put in this type of account. It would be protected from Payne.

In June 1849, Payne came to see his mother. He made her write a will. He told her to give him all of her money. Dolley wrote that will, but after Payne left, she wrote a new one. She divided the money between Payne and her niece Anna.

Dolley's Death

Shortly after she wrote her second will, Dolley became ill. She died on July 12, 1849, in Washington, D.C. Many people went to her funeral. President Zachary Taylor spoke. He said that Dolley would never be forgotten and that Dolley was

America's "first lady." This was the first time that someone used this term to describe a president's wife. Dolley was buried in the Congressional Cemetery in Washington, D.C.

Payne went to court to fight Dolley's new will. He wanted all of his mother's money. The court jury said no. In 1852, Payne died of typhoid fever in a Washington hotel.

Richard D. Cutts, Dolley's nephew, had been in California when Dolley died. When he returned to Washington, D.C., he was surprised to find that she was buried in the Congressional Cemetery there. At the time of her death, no one had thought about burying her at Montpelier. Cutts helped arrange for Dolley's grave to be moved to Montpelier. In 1858, her grave was placed there next to James' grave.

Dolley's Name

In the late 1800s, companies began to use Dolley's name to advertise. Her name was on bakeries and dairies. By the 1920s, Dolley's name was on everything from dishes and shoes to ice cream and popcorn. Most companies spelled her name Dolly. Today, her name is still seen on Dolly Madison Bakery products, including sweet rolls and doughnuts.

TIMELINE

Chronology of Dolley's Life

Born in North Carolina

Moves to Philadelphia with family

Marries John Todd

John Payne Todd is born.

William Temple Todd is born.

John Todd (husband) and William Todd die.

Marries James Madison

The Madisons move to Montpelier.

| 1768 | 1783 | 1790 | 1792 | 1793 | 1794 | 1797 | 1800 |

Historical Events

Philadelphia becomes the capital of the United States.

Montpelier

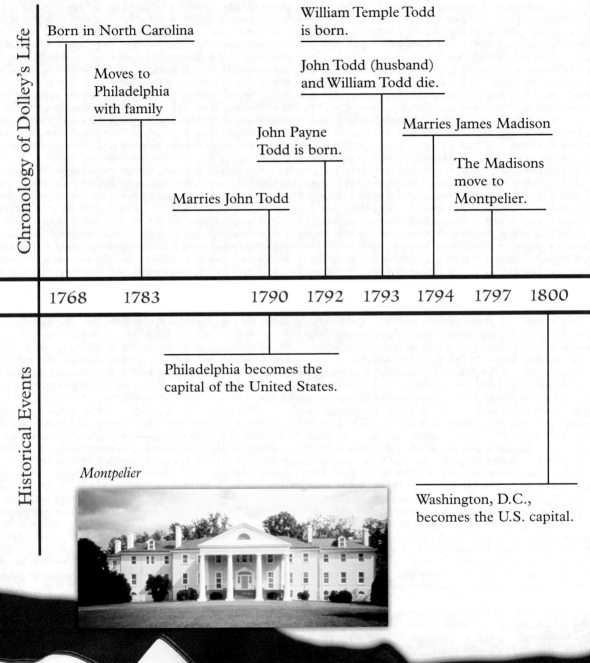

Washington, D.C., becomes the U.S. capital.

The Madisons move to
Washington, D.C.

Begins serving as hostess for
Thomas Jefferson

Moves to Washington, D.C.
with niece Anna

Sells Montpelier

Husband James Madison
dies on June 28.

Dies in
Washington,
D.C., on July 12

Becomes first
lady when James
is elected
president

The Madisons
return to
Montpelier.

| 1808 | 1814 | 1817 | 1836 | 1837 | 1844 | 1846 | 1849 |

James Madison is
elected president.

James Monroe is
elected president.

The first
telegraph
message is sent.

The British burn
Washington, D.C.

The Mexican War
begins as the United
States and Mexico fight
over land.

The Treaty of Ghent ends the
War of 1812.

James Madison is reelected president; the
United States declares war on Great Britain.

Glossary

Baked Alaska (BAYKT ul-LASS-kuh)—a slice of cake covered with ice cream and a mixture of stiffly beaten egg whites and sugar called meringue, warmed in an oven until the meringue is cooked

candelabra (kan-duh-LAH-bruh)—holders for more than one candle

Constitution (kon-stuh-TOO-shuhn)—the written system of laws of the United States that state people's rights and what the government can do

contagious (kuhn-TAY-juhss)—able to be spread by contact

debtor's prison (DET-urz PRIZ-uhn)—a jail in early America where people would be held until they could pay their bills

first lady (FURST LAY-dee)—the title given to the woman who serves as hostess for the president, usually the president's wife

meetinghouse (MEE-ting-houss)—a place where Quakers held meetings, worship, weddings, and other events

snuff (SNUHF)—powdered tobacco that people inhale through their noses

typhoid fever (TYE-foid FEE-vur)—a disease caused by bacteria, marked by fever, headache, and swelling of the stomach; typhoid fever can cause death.

For Further Reading

Haberle, Susan E. *The War of 1812.* Let Freedom Ring. Mankato, Minn.: Bridgestone Books, 2003.

Kelley, Brent P. *James Madison: Father of the Constitution.* Revolutionary War Leaders. Philadelphia: Chelsea House Publishers, 2001.

Klingel, Cynthia Fitterer, and Robert B. Noyed. *Dolley Madison: First Lady.* Chanhassen, Minn.: Child's World, 2003.

Patrick, Jean L. S. *Dolley Madison.* History Maker Bios. Minneapolis: Lerner Publications, 2002.

Pflueger, Lynda. *Dolley Madison: Courageous First Lady.* Historical American Biographies. Springfield, N.J.: Enslow Publishers, 1999.

Shulman, Holly Cowan, and David B. Mattern. *Dolley Madison: Her Life, Letters, and Legacy.* The Library of American Lives and Times. New York: PowerPlus Books, 2003.

Places of Interest

Greensboro Historical Museum

130 Summit Avenue
Greensboro, NC 27401
The Greensboro Historical museum contains a collection of items belonging to Dolley Madison and replicas of two of her dresses.

James Madison Museum

129 Caroline Street
Orange, VA 22960-1532
The James Madison Museum contains papers, personal items, and furnishings of the Madisons. A museum of farm history here also honors James, who was considered a fine farmer.

Montpelier: The Home of James Madison

11407 Constitution Highway
Montpelier Station, VA 22957
Visitors to the Madisons' home can tour the estate and view exhibits about the Madisons' lives.

Smithsonian National Museum of American History

Behring Center
14th Street and Constitution
   Avenue, NW
Washington, D.C. 20560
The First Ladies exhibit contains the gowns first ladies wore to inaugural balls. The exhibit also has information about how the role of first ladies has changed.

Internet Sites

Do you want to learn more about Dolley Madison?
Visit the FACT HOUND at *http://www.facthound.com*

FACT HOUND can track down many sites to help you.
All the FACT HOUND sites are hand-selected
by Capstone Press editors. FACT HOUND will fetch the best,
most accurate information to answer your questions.

IT IS EASY! IT IS FUN!
1) Go to *http://www.facthound.com*
2) Type in: 0736815511
3) Click on "FETCH IT" and
   FACT HOUND will put you
   on the trail of several helpful links.

You can also search by subject or book title. So, relax
and let our pal FACT HOUND do the research for you!

Index